W9-AAE-070

EXCEPTIONAL
AFRICAN AMERICANS

BARACK OBAMA

First African-American President

Charlotte Taylor
and
Stephen Feinstein

Enslow Publishing
101 W. 23rd Street
Suite 240
New York, NY 10011
USA

enslow.com

Words to Know

adventure—An exciting happening.

custom—Something that a person or group does repeatedly over a long period of time.

Hawaii—A US state made up of a group of islands in the Pacific Ocean.

Honolulu—The capital city of Hawaii.

housing projects—Groups of apartment houses for poor people to live in.

Indonesia—A country in Southeast Asia.

Jakarta—The capital city of Indonesia.

Kenya—A country in East Africa bordering on the Indian Ocean.

race—A group of people that share the same traits.

senator—A person who is elected to represent an area by voting and making laws.

Contents

Barack Obama

CHAPTER 1

Early Days

When Barack Obama was born, many people thought his parents had an unusual marriage. His mother was white and his father was black. Some people did not approve of white and black people marrying. But the country was changing, and ideas about **race** were changing too. One day, almost fifty years later, there would be another change: the first black president of the United States.

Barack Hussein Obama was born on August 4, 1961, in **Honolulu, Hawaii**. Barack's father, who was also named Barack, had come to the United States from **Kenya** to go to college. He met Barack's mother, Ann Dunham, while both of them were students at the University of Hawaii.

Young Barry

Barack and Ann called their son Barry. They lived with Ann's parents, Stanley and Madelyn. Barry called his grandfather Gramps. He called his grandmother Toot, the Hawaiian word for "grandmother."

When Barry's father finished college, he left Hawaii. His marriage to Ann ended. Barry did not

Barack Says:

"It's...the hope of a skinny kid with a funny name who believes that America has a place for him, too."

understand why his father had left. So Barry grew up feeling that something was missing.

When Barry was little, he spent many days at the beach. There he learned how to swim and body surf. Gramps had a friend who had a small fishing boat. The man took Gramps and Barry spearfishing in the ocean.

Barry, four years old, plays with Gramps at the beach.

CHAPTER 2

A New Land

In 1965, Barry's mother married a student from **Indonesia** named Lolo Soetoro. A couple of years later, Barry and his mother went to live in Indonesia with Lolo.

The family lived near the city of **Jakarta**. In the backyard were chickens, ducks, and two baby crocodiles. They also had a pet gibbon, an ape, named Tata.

Lolo took Barry and Ann to visit villages in the jungle. Barry saw boys riding on water buffalo.

This boy is riding a water buffalo. Barry saw scenes like this when he lived in Indonesia.

Barack Says:

"You can't let your failures define you—you have to let your failures teach you. You have to let them show you what to do differently next time."

Barry tasted foods he had never eaten before. He tried dog meat, snake meat, and roasted grasshopper.

An Important Lesson

Barry went to school in Indonesia. He quickly learned the Indonesian language and **customs**. He also learned about what it means to be poor. Some Indonesians were rich, but many were very,

Like Barack as a child, these students are at a school in Jakarta, Indonesia.

very poor. Some people had enough to eat, while others did not know when they would eat again.

After a few years, Ann was afraid that Barry was not learning enough at school. Also, she and Lolo were not getting along very well. So in 1971, Ann and Barry moved back to Hawaii. The **adventure** was over.

This is a poor area of Jakarta. Barry saw many poor people when he lived in Indonesia.

CHAPTER 3

A Time of Change

Barry and his mother returned to Honolulu to live with his grandparents. Barry, who was now ten, started the fifth grade. That year, Barack, Barry's father, came from Africa to visit. He told Barry about Africa and his relatives there. A month later, Barack went home to Kenya. Barry never saw his father again.

Barry was a good student. In high school, he played on the school basketball team. To others, Barry seemed happy. But something was bothering him.

Barry's mother was white. His father was black. Barry did not know how he fit in. He felt different, and he felt alone.

Barack Helps Others

In 1979, Barry began studying at Occidental College in Los Angeles. While he was there, Barry learned that South Africa had a white government that was very unfair to black people. Barry spoke out against the terrible treatment of blacks in South Africa. He began to think of himself as black. He started to call himself by his Kenyan name, Barack. He was proud of the name, which means "blessing from God."

In 1981, Barack moved New York City to attend Columbia University. He graduated in 1983. For the next few years, Barack worked in Chicago helping poor people in **housing projects** make their lives better.

Many of Barack's family members came from Kenya, in East Africa.

Barack Says:

"If you're walking down the right path and you're willing to keep walking, eventually you'll make progress."

In 1988, Barack traveled to Kenya. There he met his grandmother, Sarah Hussein Obama, for the first time. He also met aunts, uncles, and cousins.

Sadly, Barack's father was no longer alive. Barack cried at his father's grave. By the time he left Kenya, Barack really knew who he was.

CHAPTER 4

From Senator to President

Barack knew he wanted to help people. He decided to go to Harvard Law School. He graduated in 1991 with the highest honors. In 1992, he married Michelle Robinson, a lawyer he had met in Chicago. They had two daughters, Malia and Sasha.

Also in 1992, Barack began working for a law firm in Chicago. He gave legal help to people who had been treated unfairly at their jobs. Barack decided he could do the most good for the most people if he went into politics. In 1996, he won an election for Illinois state **senator**. For seven years, he worked to pass laws that helped the people of Illinois.

Road to the White House

In 2004, Barack was elected to the US Senate. That same year, he gave an important speech. He said that if Americans joined together, they could make dreams come true for every parent and child.

In 2007, Barack decided to run for president. The country was ready for a change. He won the election and became the first African-American president of the United States.

Barack Says:

"Change will not come if we wait for some other person or some other time. We are the ones we've been waiting for. We are the change that we seek."

Over a million people went to Washington DC to watch Barack become president.

Barack celebrates winning the 2008 election with (left to right) Sasha, Malia, and Michelle.

Barack lives and works in the White House.

When he became president, Barack took on challenges like wars, poverty, guns, and health care. He continued his work when he was elected again in 2012.

Barack Obama has faced many challenges in his own life as well as in his job as president. But he has never stopped working to help America change for the better.

Timeline

1961—Barack Obama (Barry) is born in Honolulu, Hawaii, on August 4.

1967—Barry moves to Jakarta, Indonesia, with his mother and stepfather, Lolo Soetoro.

1971—Barry and his mother return to Hawaii. His father visits from Africa.

1979—Barry starts college. He starts to use his full first name, Barack.

1983—Barack graduates from Columbia University in New York City.

1988—Barack travels to Kenya and meets his African grandmother and other relatives.

1991—Barack graduates from Harvard Law School.

1992—Barack begins working for a law firm in Chicago. He marries Michelle Robinson.

1996—Barack wins an election for Illinois state senator.

2004—Barack gives an important speech. Barack is elected a US senator from Illinois.

2008—Barack is elected 44th president of the United States.

2009—Barack is awarded the Nobel Peace Prize.

2010—Barack signs his new health care bill. He declares the end of the war in Iraq.

2012—Barack is elected to a second term as president.

Learn More

Books

Bausum, Ann. *Our Country's Presidents.* Washington, D.C.: National Geographic, 2013.

Doak, Robin S. *Barack Obama.* New York: Scholastic, 2013.

Nichols, Catherine. *Barack Obama: Our Forty-Fourth President.* North Mankato, Minn.: Child's World, 2013.

Web Sites

kids.usa.gov/government/index.shtml
Explains the three branches of government and the election process.

whitehouse.gov/about/presidents/barackobama
Includes a biography of Barack Obama as well as links to other presidential biographies.

Index

Published in 2016 by Enslow Publishing, LLC.
101 W. 23rd Street, Suite 240, New York, NY 10011

Copyright © 2016 by Enslow Publishing, LLC.

All rights reserved.

No part of this book may be reproduced by any means without the written permission of the publisher.

Library of Congress Cataloging-in-Publication Data
Taylor, Charlotte, 1978-
 Barack Obama : first African-American president / Charlotte Taylor and Stephen Feinstein.
  pages cm. — (Exceptional African Americans)
 Summary: "A biography of US president Barack Obama"—Provided by publisher.
 Audience: Grades 4 to 6.
 Includes bibliographical references and index.
 ISBN 978-0-7660-7124-7 (library binding)
 ISBN 978-0-7660-7122-3 (pbk.)
 ISBN 978-0-7660-7123-0 (6-pack)
1. Obama, Barack—Juvenile literature. 2. Presidents—United States—Biography--Juvenile literature. 3. African American politicians—Biography—Juvenile literature. 4. Racially mixed people—United States—Biography—Juvenile literature. I. Feinstein, Stephen. II. Title.
 E908.T28 2015
 973.932092—dc23
 [B]

 2015007447

Printed in the United States of America

To Our Readers: We have done our best to make sure all Web site addresses in this book were active and appropriate when we went to press. However, the author and the publisher have no control over and assume no liability for the material available on those Web sites or on any Web sites they may link to. Any comments or suggestions can be sent by e-mail to customerservice@enslow.com.

Photo Credits: Getty Images: Bryn Campbell/The Image Bank, p. 9; Danita Delimont/Gallo Images, p. 11; Obama Presidential Campaign/AP, p. 7; Shutterstock.com: ©Toria (blue background throughout book); ©Everett Collection, pp. 1, 20; ©s_bukley, p. 4; ©Worldpics, p. 12; ©PHOTOCREO Michal Bednarek, p. 15; ©Vacclav, p. 21; ©Scott Cornell, p. 19.

Cover Credits: Shutterstock.com: ©Everett Collection (portrait of Barack Obama); ©Toria (blue background).